ARTIST BLACKSMITH SCULPTURE

The Art of Natural Metalwork

I have been forging metal for over 20 years, producing unique sculptural metalwork for private homes and gardens as well as public spaces, galleries, parks and museums. Over the years I've been lucky enough to exhibit my work across the length and breadth of the UK.

Collected here are many of my best pieces from the last two decades, as well as a look at the art of sculptural metalwork itself and the skills involved.

You will also find some of my design sketches and ideas, plus a look at how other smiths around the world work, with a unique look into the dark corners of the blacksmith's shop.

With thanks to Thomas Moulton and Mike Kelly.

More of David Freedman's work can be seen at:
www.davidfreedmansculpture.com

Details of David's writing can be found at:
www.stuntcrow.com

All photography © David Freedman except where otherwise credited.

Contents

1. When Metal Comes Alive
2. Furniture as Sculpture
3. Design and Detail
4. Decorative Gates
5. The Forge
6. Figurative Sculpture
7. Insect Sculpture
8. Copper and Water

When Metal Comes Alive

I believe that if sculpture takes something from the landscape, it should give something back. For countless centuries people have been crumbling fragments of metal from rocks and scorching them to liquid, only to forge them into art that has such strength and permanence that it can endure for millennia. This gives the artist a unique responsibility to enhance the setting into which the sculpture is placed.

As an artist blacksmith and sculptor I see my work as a process of interpreting nature and synthesising aspects of it into something new, something never seen before, with a balance of beauty and strength but crucially with great sympathy for the site in which it will be displayed.

For me the evocative landscape of the United Kingdom has always been a source of inspiration, but though many of my sculptures are quite literal in subject, they are rarely direct representations of nature. When I was asked by the Forestry Commission to create a piece of sculpture for the Wyre Forest, an ancient woodland hunting ground frequented by kings since medieval times, I chose the image of a stag standing still amongst the trees to represent both the history and the tranquility of the forest. I wanted the piece to be discovered by visitors much as they might chance upon a living deer. This influenced the decision to structure the piece around a see-through framework rather than make it solid. I also designed the piece to be far larger than life-size but not to appear too big. The fallow deer is actually a relatively small species with an adult standing only three feet to the shoulder, but though I wanted it to be somewhat hidden in the woods, once found it should have striking impact. The size of the sculpture (around ten feet in overall height) gives it an other-worldly quality and this is enhanced by the galvanised finish on the wrought iron framework, which is etched with a mild acid to give it a mottled, leaden patina.

I used the same technique to create my Pictish Boar sculpture for a woodland setting in southern Scotland, though in this case the inspiration did not come from the animal itself, but from an iron-age depiction of a boar cut into the

Opposite: Fallow Deer Buck, Wyre Forest, Gloucestershire (2012)

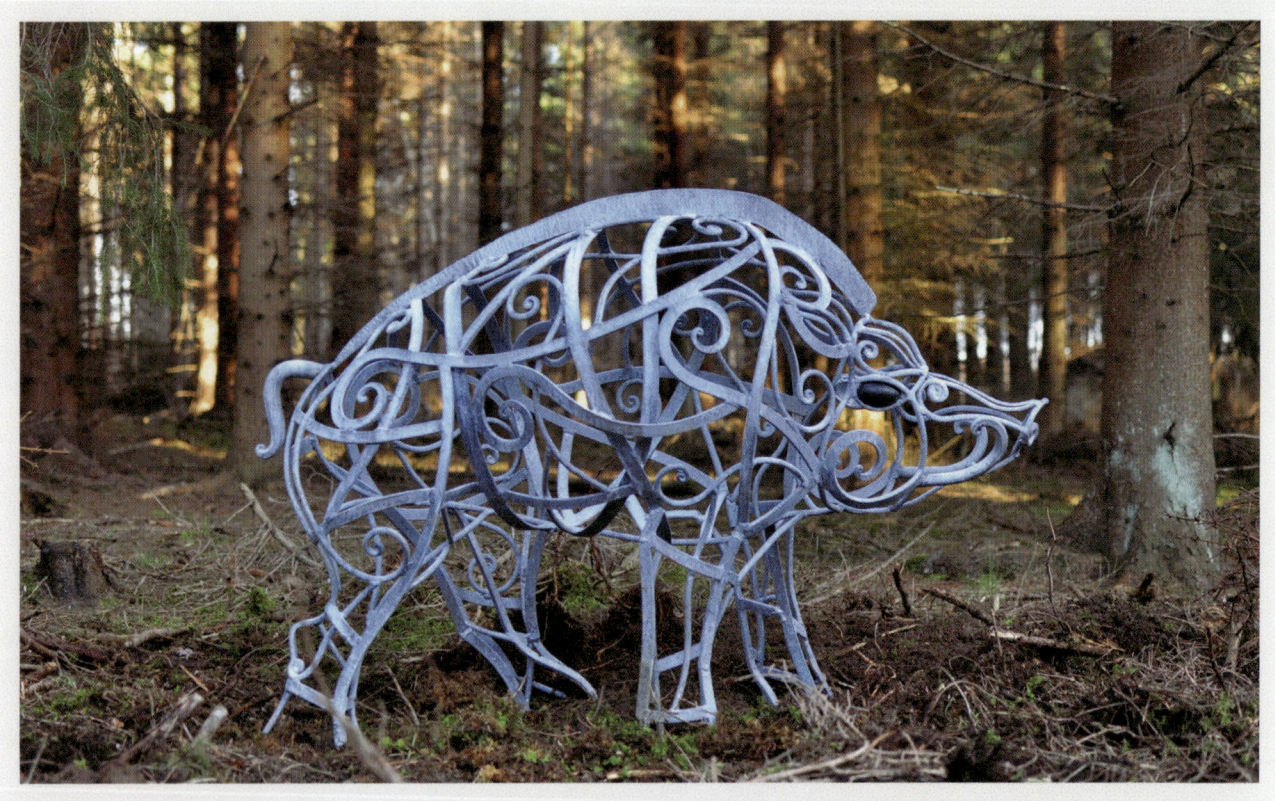

Knocknagael Boar Stone in the Highlands of Scotland by Pictish people who left few other clues to their identity and culture. The challenge here was not in modelling an animal in metal, but rather to bring an ancient two-dimensional line drawing to life in metal whilst keeping it sympathetic to its environment.

At the same site I was asked to make some sculpted woodlice to be placed in a tree. I wanted them to have a creepy feel that would appeal to adults but especially to children. This was simply a case of making them extra large in size, making something small and familiar weird and surprising.

Above: The Pictish Boar (2014), Butterdean Wood, East Lothian, Scotland

This also serves to highlights another important function of sculpture, to make us look again at the familiar and see it in a new light.

Just as an aged finish on galvanised wrought iron gives a timeless and natural quality to a sculpture, so stainless steel lends an unwavering permanence. Its brilliant finish, if handled with due care, can last indefinitely. I have found that combining this with the ever changing patina of copper creates an interesting contrast, standing out from its setting and yet ageing and changing like a part of nature.

My *Wasp on Flower* sculpture added a natural local stone plinth to this combination of metals, rooting it in the landscape. Both the stone and the copper elements will darken, age and develop, while the stainless steel will remain constant.

Every so often I feel that a commission calls for the use of one metal alone. Fountains and water features lend themselves to the use of copper which is easily shaped, beaten, folded and indented in detail.

Left: Woodlice (2014) Photo by Niall Benvie

The natural properties of copper cause it to age in response to the weather and contact with water, at first turning it darker and then eventually oxidising it to a striking verdigris or blue-green patina, a process which can take years, helping to blur the edge between the static permanence of the artwork and the constant flux of nature.

Even though I don't seek to copy nature and much of my work is part fantasy, I feel it's important to echo the complexities of natural forms and not to take the risk of a sculpture looking simple or clumsy in its setting.

When asked to produce a dragonfly sculpture to be placed in a pond, I decided that stainless steel would best catch reflections and bounce light up from the piece, and that other metals in this case would be a distraction. Unusually for me, I took the decision to have the wings processed at a local waterjet cutting shop where water is fired at very high pressure through a fine nozzle to cut metals with great precision and no distortion or heating.

Right: Wasp (2013), Copper and Stainless Steel - Cheshire, UK

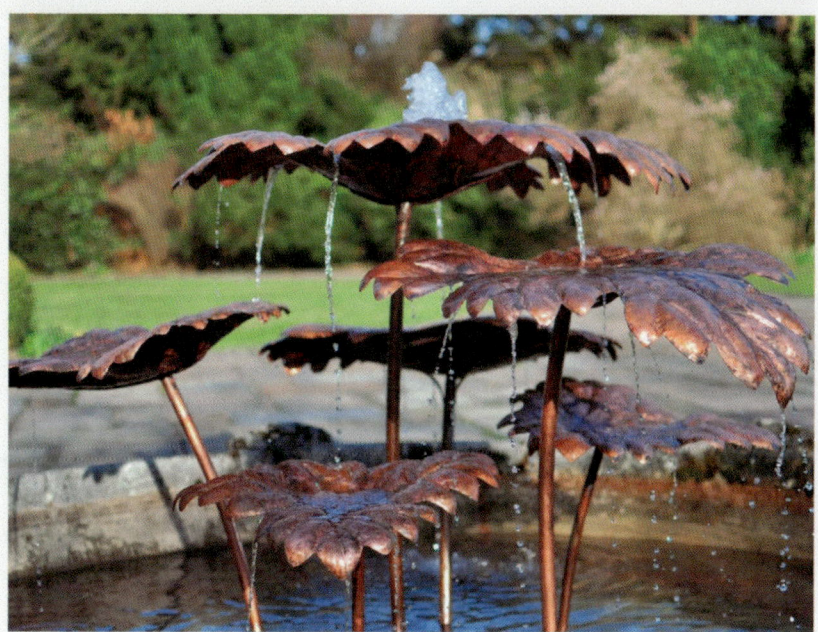

They were able to digitise and scale my original design and reproduce it faithfully, helping to capture the intricacies of the insect wings.

Setting is everything for sculpture and it sometimes takes a leap of the imagination to try to envisage the unfinished piece that sits on the workshop bench in a lush country garden or waterside landscape. I was amazed when a client showed me with pride where they had placed a sculptural garden chair they bought from me the previous year. It was inside. To my great surprise it looked good against a backdrop of timber clad walls, well lit from above in the entrance to their home, but I was struck most of all at how different it seemed. Its colour, its weight, the impact it had and even its size appeared totally changed.

Top: Dragonfly 2012, Wyre Forest, Gloucestershire
Set in a pond within the forest landscape. Wyre Forest is a huge and ancient woodland.

Left: Detail of a copper fountain with Gunnera leaf design, 2013 Set in the grounds of a Georgian Manor in the beautiful landscape of the Lake District National Park.

Furniture as Sculpture

Garden seating has a unique role in the landscape, both as a sculptural feature in itself and as a focal point in the landscape from which to view and enjoy the surroundings.

When exhibiting my work at Hidcote Manor Garden, "an Arts and Crafts masterpiece in the north Cotswolds", I was asked by a helpful curator if I would like them to place notices on my chairs and benches to inform visitors not to sit down. I explained that in my opinion, a sculpture designed as seating must be sat on to be fully appreciated, but that positioning the seat would be key. Once the exhibition opened I witnessed many people sitting on my benches to enjoy the intricate beauty of the gardens in bloom, at first not even looking at the bench. But in every case, when they rose to continue their visit, they would turn to admire the seat, often reaching out to touch the metal again.

It's clear that, in my own work at least, the landscape comes first. It is the source of ideas, the visual cue for details and designs. The way the metal sits in its final position is all important. I focus less on technique and more on result. I feel that it's necessary to persuade the material in any way possible to take a form that will engage with the land in which it sits, to be enjoyed for years to come.

I often use wood for benches and chairs as it provides warmth and comfort, but I like the ageing process of timber and ideally I would like to source it from somewhere where it has been able to weather naturally. As this is rarely possible, I have found ways to accelerate the natural process, sometimes using natural oils and liming wax. I tend to use oak as I know that it will endure, hopefully as long as the metalwork of the seat and will require little or no care long term as it hardens as it ages. It also has character.

Opposite: *Leaf design bench in galvanised and acid etched wrought iron. Oak seat with limed finish.*

Right: Reed design Bench 2014 designed and made for one of the largest private gardens in central London (after Buckingham Palace of course!). The simple 'reed' design has a woven slatted seat and is galvanised and then acid etched. Though my seats are sculptural, I always ensure they are comfortable to sit on by raking the back and subtly angling the seat to slope backwards.

Right bottom: Oak Leaf design bench with English Oak seat 2010 The oak came from a tree that blew down in a local village and was then processed by a nearby salvage yard. The seat is treated with oils and waxes which can either be maintained to the same finish over the years or allowed to fade to a natural grey, in which state oak can remain strong and stable for a very long time.

Opposite: Oberon's Chair 2009 This chair was named Oberon's chair after its fantasy quality. Here it is shown, aptly, at a gallery exhibition in Henley in Arden, Shakespeare Country.
The wrought iron frame has been galvanised and then paint finished and the seat is burr oak, waxed and polished.

Above: Acer Leaf Bench 2012, Galvanised wrought iron and limed oak seat. Pictured at Mill Forge, Cheshire.

Opposite Left: Leaf Chair 2013
The beautiful gardens of England in summer lend themselves perfectly to decorative seating, offering rest, space for reflection and hopefully sympathetic adornment. The leaf chair is shown here in a late summer exhibition at Hidcote Manor Garden, surrounded by seemingly endless borders of colour.

Opposite Right: Forget-me-not chair displayed in the grounds of Sudeley Castle in Gloucestershire, a beguiling 15th century manor house, once home to Queen Katherine Parr, the last of Henry VIII's wives and the only one to survive him.

Nature usually provides the initial inspiration for a piece of work and in this case I was growing peas in my garden and became fascinated with the tendrils and shoots that supported the plants and took the weight of the pods. It occurred to me how metal-like they were and how well the forms would be suited to forged stems.

Opposite Top Left: Pea pod sculpture detail.

Opposite Bottom Left: Large Leaf design throne with limed oak seat.

Opposite Right: Pea pod chair with oak seat.

Left: Tree bench in painted wrought iron and oak boards.

Design and Detail

Design is key to decorative metalwork. This may seem an obvious statement, but over the years I have found that many craftspeople are more led by training and technique than design, asking first 'what can I achieve using this method' rather than 'what is the image I am seeking to create', a question which leads the artist to find techniques that will achieve the desired result so that the final product is not compromised.

In many ways I have lagged behind many of my fellow smiths in my skill set and my technical abilities, all of which I have struggled to learn through necessity, having no formal training or the grounding of an apprenticeship. In fact many traditional smiths are unhappy about the free use of the title of blacksmith, adopted by artists and fabricators who choose to work in metal, but lack many of the core skills. A rule of thumb for many is the ability to fire-weld, the ancient art of joining metals using forge and anvil alone and without the need for electric or gas welding. Fortunately I can scrape through this test with my limited experience of forging blades and a few successful welds, practised to justify the theft of my title. The title Artist Blacksmith, though worryingly grand, is an apt description, both to excuse the modern crop from the need to prove ourselves as farriers and nailmakers, and to highlight this new attitude to the anvil, which in essence is design-led.

For me, pen and paper can never be replaced. I am not a luddite when it comes to new technology and often make use of processes such as high pressure water jet cutting, galvanising etc, but I believe that the authenticity of hand made work is lost when the perfection of the computer is involved in design. What people seem to admire about the blacksmith's work is that every detail is individual, no two scrolls are the same and there is an organic feel, brought to life by the crude material we so love to heat and beat and bend.

Much of my work depends upon the eye to bring design to life. The hand and the hammer need only fulfil their roles in following the sketch. This is why I have to make my ideas work on paper before they ever enter the gloom of the forge.

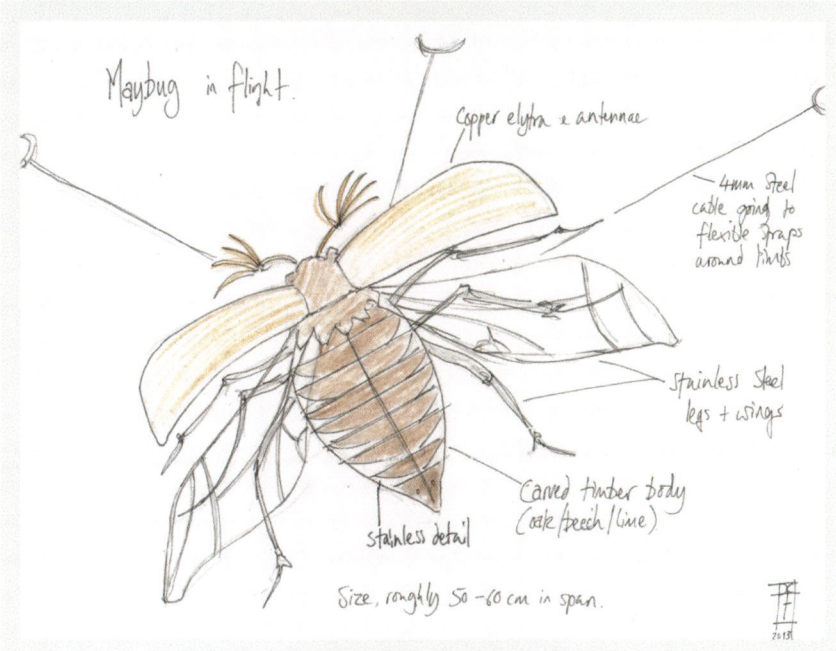

The flat image on paper, though a vital step, often poses serious challenges. Initially I am content with the concept, but then, when the scrap of paper enters the workshop and I stand, tea in hand, staring at an empty bench, the puzzle of how this is going to be achieved begins.

In the case of this cockchafer beetle destined to be suspended between trees in a wood in Scotland, the sketch was transformed into a carved lump of oak wood, clad in a thin skin of stainless steel and then encased in a detailed carapace of copper. The final piece was hung between two mighty pine trunks at about 20ft above ground, using thin stainless steel wire cables and flexible straps.

Opposite Top Left: Detail from a bramble gate.
Opposite Top Right: Flower for a gate
Opposite Bottom Left: Pea pod sculpture
Opposite Bottom Right: Detail from a bench

Left Top: Maybug Sculpture 2014 For the Woodland Trust, Scotland.
Left Bottom: Maybug Sculpture design.

23

Decorative Gates

Perhaps the smallest gate I ever made was for the largest garden. One of the largest private gardens in London in fact, second only to that of Buckingham Palace. Set within the bounds of Regent's Park, passers by on the other side of the Regent's canal would be forgiven for thinking that this softly sloping paradise of pathways and specimen trees, flowers and palms was a section of the park they had not yet discovered. And yet in this setting that had everything, it was not opulence or finery that was to be portrayed in the gate, but subtlety, silence and secrecy.

The gate (p.32) was to be placed in a narrow gap within a wild yew hedge that overhung to form a small arch. Its role would be to invite you into a secret hideaway, a tranquil escape. I kept the design simple, and the colour black, so that the gate would melt away into the foliage, becoming a silhouette. I used just enough floral detail and decoration to hint at what lay beyond.

A gate is a pause. A full stop. It causes us to consider where we are. Whose territory are we entering? What lies within. It can be both a barrier and an invitation, a welcome or a warning. On grander properties a gate may be seen as a status symbol for the occupant, but for me this has much less to do with the design than the property itself. Of course it should reflect some of the desires and ideals of its patron, but essentially it should always be an artistic and architectural enhancement.

In design terms a gate is a dream job. It is largely two dimensional save for a little texture, it creates its own frame on the page as it does on the workbench, and of all sculptural works it is one that a drawing can truly capture, meaning that the client gets a very good taste of what they are getting in advance.

The art of the gate, as I hope you will see, is all in the design. The drawing comes first and the technical worries in the workshop whilst staring at it thinking 'How am I going to make this?' are secondary.

Opposite: Round Acer Leaf Gate, 2013 - Private house in Mobberly, Cheshire.

Top: A large single gate designed for a Georgian manor house in Cumbria. Designed to echo the 'decaying grandeur' of the existing gate posts. The details were intended to create the illusion of a formal gate that has become overgrown.

Bottom: Original design drawing for the 'decaying grandeur gate'

Opposite: Design details from the gate. Mostly 'fictional' flowers and leaf patterns, perhaps reflecting Victorian romanticism.

It can be tricky to make a gate sympathetic to its setting without it being mundane, or worse still clumsy or unsuitable. In a landscape such as this, I felt that a natural feel must prevail, but that flourishes of the Georgian and later Victorian styles of some of the surrounding architecture could be evoked in some of the more outlandish details, with larger than life trumpet flowers, scroll-like tendrils and sprouting finials. The centrepiece is a huge imagined flower *(opposite, bottom right)* with a natural feel but not based on any real flower. The key factor was to make this a worthy match for the enormous pineapple tops on the posts.

I was asked to design a set of gates for a tiny treasure of a public garden in the centre of Norwich. The Plantation Garden is the site of an old chalk quarry that was transformed by a wealthy Victorian businessman in 1856 called Henry Trevor. He spent years building elaborate palm houses, Italianate fountains and high terraces with balustrades, all within the 3 acre site. He also created medieval follies like fragments of some lost monastery.

Sadly, the prime reason for the gates was for security as local youths had recently seen the garden as a hangout point and had caused damage after hopping over the wooden gates. The trustees wanted something unclimbable that would be an enhancement rather than an ugly defence, so I set about making something suitably floral and appropriately eccentric.

There were some that felt the gates should be a traditional Victorian design, but I felt that Mr Trevor would have approved.

Top: Plantation Gates, shortly after installation 2014

Bottom: Original design sketch

Top: Tudor Manor House Gates, Chelford, Cheshire 2010

The lightest details on this set of grand entrance gates turned out to be the most important.

The property was a 16th century wattle and daub manor with its own small lake and wooded grounds. Some of the bolder details, the simple fleur de lys and the star and chequered patterns, were lifted directly from the high status timber work in the gables of the building itself. But the elements that the client personally requested, the honeysuckle flower and the wisteria flowing across the top, were to give this otherwise imposing barrier a softness and an organic feel.

Bottom: Tudor Manor Gates installed.

At nearly 3m high to the centre, this is an imposing set of gates, largely traditional in design but with some lighter natural detail to soften the impact. The gates were automated with an intercom system. The posts were designed to be proportionally large without appearing too solid or heavy. A small crane had to be used to lift the gates into position.

I have included the above designs despite the fact that the gate was never actually commissioned. I think they illustrate the myriad ways that a design can be tackled.

Top left shows the most traditional of the three, in structure at least. Strong Victorian scrollwork defines the character of the scheme, though it is overlaid with more organic detail which contradicts the apparent symmetry.

Top Middle: More overall solidity is achieved by the use of leaves and larger scrollwork patterns. Though the pattern is more repetitive it seems more complex and dynamic.

Top Right: Using a totally different style which owes much to Art Nouveau, the confined shape of the stone archway is made to feel more open and inviting. The lack of a solid top frame gives a more wild and loose feel even though this is a symmetrical design.

In all of these designs, the solid lower section of plate was a requirement to keep in small pets and keep out rabbits, but an interesting addition to the design rather than an afterthought.

In general terms I find that there is a balance between the more wild and natural elements which I clearly love to include, and the symmetry and structure of traditional ironwork around which even the most eccentric designs are based. Symmetry offers strength and draws the eye into the centre, leading us to enter. Asymmetry offers a glimpse of something else. A little surprise. A reminder that structure is not everything and that nature's symmetry is rarely exact if there is any at all.

Opposite: Design idea next to final gate. This design started with little structure or symmetry but was eventually enhanced by the addition of a light and subtle structure in the form of a faux trellis, allowing more freedom of line.

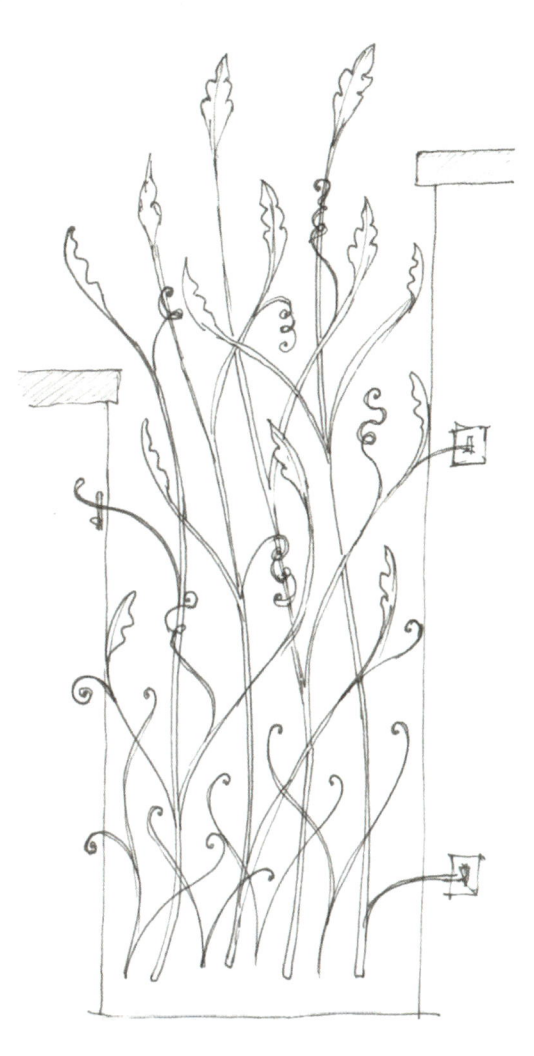

I have mentioned how gates are a design dream in that they are sketches in themselves. Solid embodiments of a page of design. This is even more true of smaller gates that don't have the expanse to paint a larger more complex picture and so rely on a simpler idea, sometimes a sketch based on natural forms, sometimes simply a pattern. Context and background are all important to achieve a balance between a stand out design and one that blends with its setting.

Opposite Left: Wave Gate 2009 - Cheshire
A simple design of hand beaten shapes, to give the feel of a natural material, such as wooden slats or bamboo.

Opposite Right: Secret Garden Gate, 2011 - London
A hidden portal into a small oasis of calm in a huge park-like garden in central London. Again, a relatively simple design.

Top Left: Reed Gate, 2009 - Cotswolds
This gate exemplifies the sketch-like properties of a gate. In this case, the gate was so light as to almost disappear into the planting of the garden, but to be enjoyed from the pathways and at close quarters.

Top Middle: Pear Tree Gate, 2013 - Cotswolds
When asked to make a gate for Pear Tree Cottage, there was only one realistic design choice, and the form of an espalier pear tree on its trellis lent itself perfectly to the design.

Top Right: Laid Hedge Gate, 2010 - Worcestershire
Ihave always admired the form of laid hedges, especially in winter when the structure can be seen. Because they are made in this way as a barrier to livestock, the structure is perfect for a gate and has a very organic feel.

I often use leaves in my design as they add interest and solidity to the simple line of a gate. They can also add texture and pattern. I tend to use leaf forms that I see locally in the countryside. Sometimes I forge them in the traditional way and in other cases I cut the basic shape from steel plate and then add texture with a variety of purpose made forming tools that I have developed over the years.

Top: Wild Gates Design
Some design ideas come from loose freehand sketches such as this and then every effort is made to keep the gate itself fluid and organic in design.

Bottom: Wild Gates 2010
The design includes sycamore, hazel, ash and oak leaves all drawn from the British countryside

Opposite Left: Foliage Gate 2010
This gate was made for a garden in which I noticed many multiple lobed leaves which I included. Horse chestnut, Castor oil plant and Japanese maple.

Opposite Right: Vine Gate 2015
Vine leaves have a decorative shape and the tendrils lend themselves well to forged metal.

I often work with garden and landscape designers, creating architectural work and sculpture to enhance elements of their design layouts. In this situation the metalwork needed to reflect the naturalistic style of planting and the rugged landscape of the Peak District.

The design is based on fern fronds and swaying grasses and reeds but retains some abstract features of a traditional style metal design with scrollwork and in places a formal structure, though this is without straight lines. The top rails of the balustrade and side bars of the gate are vertical and horizontal but wiggle like vines or tendrils, and the top of the gate opens to no structure at all, mimicking the flowerheads and grasses in the surrounding design scheme.

Opposite: Garden viewed through my fern design gate.

Left Top: Design drawing showing balustrade and gate

Left Bottom: Metalwork viewed through the foliage.

(Photos by kind permission and garden design by David Keegan)

Above: Kelp Gates, Helston, Cornwall 2013
I was delighted to be asked to create a set of gates for a large art deco property overlooking the Helford River on the Lizard Peninsula in Cornwall. Though the entrance to the drive was neither in view of the house nor the sea, I wanted to encapsulate the era of art deco to give a flavour of the house that lay beyond, and also add a seaside element. I experimented with forging various seaweeds and plants and eventually took the form of strands of kelp which lent themselves perfectly to being forged in steel. The structure of the gates would essentially be a simple art-deco linear form with swept back post tops, but the kelp would then be woven fairly randomly between. The result is of course not an art deco style in itself, but I hope still retains some of the feel of the period. My aim too was to capture something of the exotic in a remote corner of Britain where there is a familiar Englishness but also a taste of the continent.

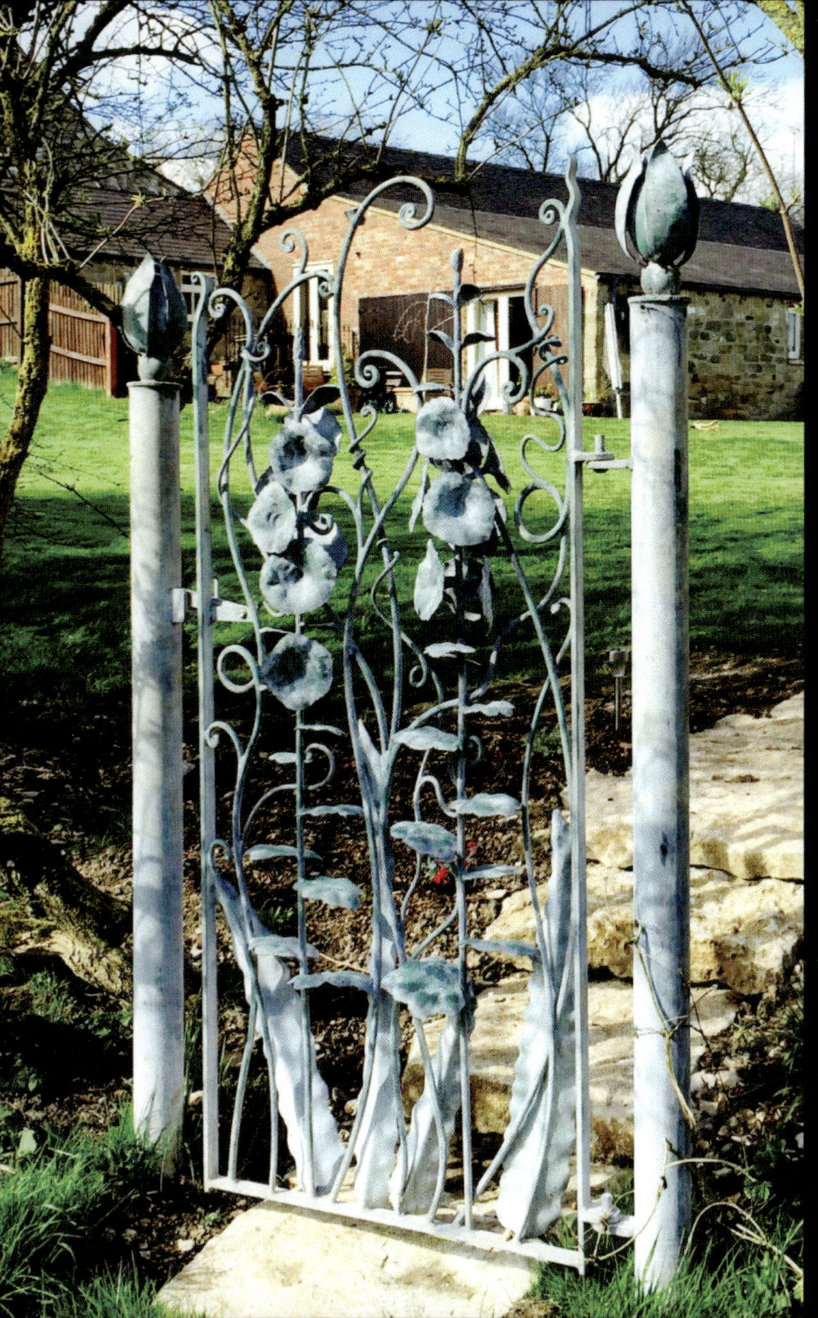

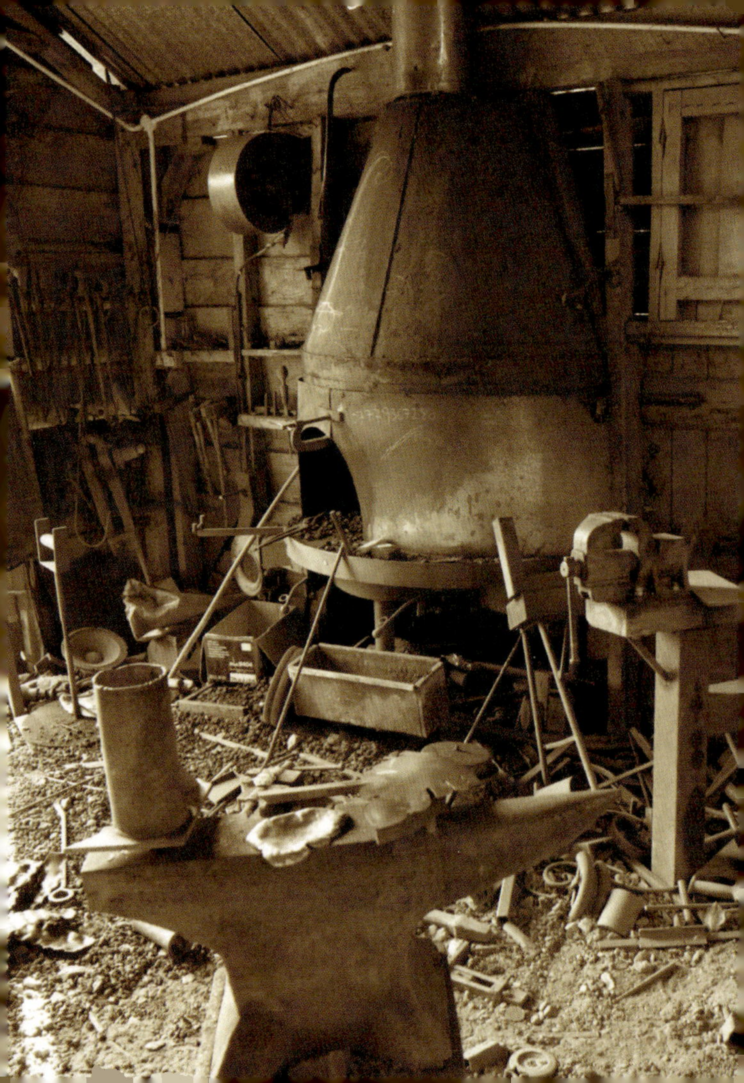

The Forge

The unmistakeable smell of the smithy, scorched coke, sweat and metallic dust from a damp earth floor hit me before I could see through the dimness on first entering Mark Cross Forge in Sussex, southern England twenty years ago. Everything that should have repelled me, the noise and the grime, the fire and the sparks only drew me in further and I was hooked.

Giles Blakeley the blacksmith was only 8 years my senior but one of a dying breed of fully trained and apprenticed blacksmiths at the time in the UK. His creative brand of hand forged work proved popular in the affluent counties surrounding London, but blacksmithing was at a turning point, poised between the age-old trade that made every hand tool, sharpened the scythe and the plough, and the new era that recognised its skills as an art and hailed the smith as an artisan to visit for something special. Something unique. Like many other people since, I became inspired to set up my own forge and moved back to the Cheshire village where I grew up.

The blacksmith's shop in my village has probably been a fixture since the iron age began over two thousand years ago. The river bridge is an important crossing point that would have been used by the Romans to move between two nearby salt mining towns and it seems likely that there would have been a smith at hand who could fix cart wheels and sharpen tools. Records from November 1824 show that numerous trades existed in the village then; blacksmith, wheelwright, weaver, tailor, gamekeeper and victualler among others. These days myself and an artist potter are the only tradespeople left, the car allowing others the relative freedom to skip the six miles into the nearest town for work, with many travelling the near 30 miles to the city.

In 2006 I was lucky enough to meet Stan Farrall, a smith who had served his apprenticeship in the village smithy in the 1920s and retired in the 1970s. Nearly blind and walking with great care, he had insisted on visiting my smithy and seemed delighted to see that the forge and anvil were still firm fixtures.

Opposite: The Forge, photo by Andy Meany

working on everything from cartwheels to farm machinery and even providing a funeral service.

The decline of traditional blacksmithing was inevitable with changes in mass manufacturing, mechanisation and the cost of labour, but the inherent adaptability of the smith's skills has meant that they have always found a niche and over recent decades the artist blacksmith has emerged.

The final chapter of 1971 classic, "The Village Blacksmith" by Ronald Webber is entitled 'The End of the Road', lamenting the demise of the village smith and charting his decline, citing examples such as the mechanisation of nail making and hand tool production and the rise of

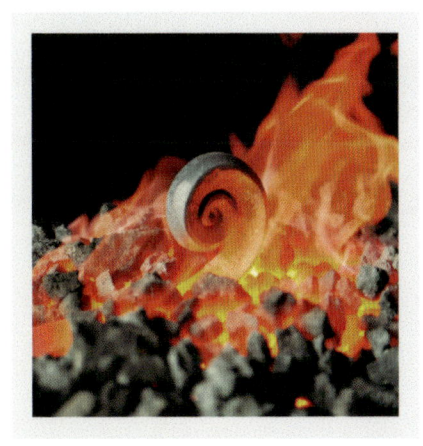

This perhaps marks the lowest point of the smith's art and any revival seemed unlikely, yet in the States, the smith's craft seems to have always held some value.

Pioneers like Samuel Yellin, an early exponent of what we might now call artist blacksmithing, worked in Philadelphia in the early 1900s, a renowned master blacksmith but he also attended art school, for a time even teaching classes at the Museum School of Industrial Art. Following in the tradition of medieval smiths of Europe, where ironwork for cathedrals and royal buildings had become highly decorative, Yellin produced stunningly artistic work that took architectural ironwork way beyond simple functionality.

The artistic side of blacksmithing is what first appealed to me and drove me to want to create unique pieces of metalwork, progressing gradually to this by making the things people wanted and needed but trying to add a twist of individuality. This helped me to build a more artistic reputation, eventually being able to specialise in more sculptural work. Most blacksmiths in the UK are now either specialists or like myself they tend towards more creative, design led work. But there is undoubtedly a new resurgence of interest in this ancient trade, both in the United Kingdom and the United States.

Now, more than ever, in the age of information, the ancient craftsman is able to share in a wealth of knowledge and experience regardless of oceans and borders. Last year I was visited by Tom Zimmer, an Alaskan farmer with an interest in blacksmithing, on a visit to the UK with his family and curious to visit a workshop like mine. Tom was first introduced to blacksmithing when a local farrier and metalworker offered to make him a farm entrance sign and gates: "It did not take long for me to see the many utilitarian aspects of blacksmithing."

Above: David at the forge in Cheshire

"The ability to fix tools was great but the ability to modify/alter tools to your needs was truly eye opening. I am fascinated by it as it allows me to create a tool but it requires me to loosen up and add form to that function"

For Tom, blacksmithing represents an extra craft to add to the many homesteading skills taught at Calypso Farm and Ecology Center. Like myself, Tom has not had formal training in blacksmithing other than occasional short courses, but "I have met blacksmiths from all over, male and female, old and young and they have always been so gracious to open up their smithies to show me skills. So here is yet another wonderful attribute of the trade, building community and sharing traditions."

Perhaps the best illustration of the camaraderie that exists within the trade can be seen on St Clement's Day. An hour away from my workshop over in Derbyshire, an ancient tradition is being revived. On the 23rd of November, smiths from the local area and beyond meet for an annual St Clement's Day feast.

Right: Photo by Kirsty Thompson By kind permission Cheshire Life

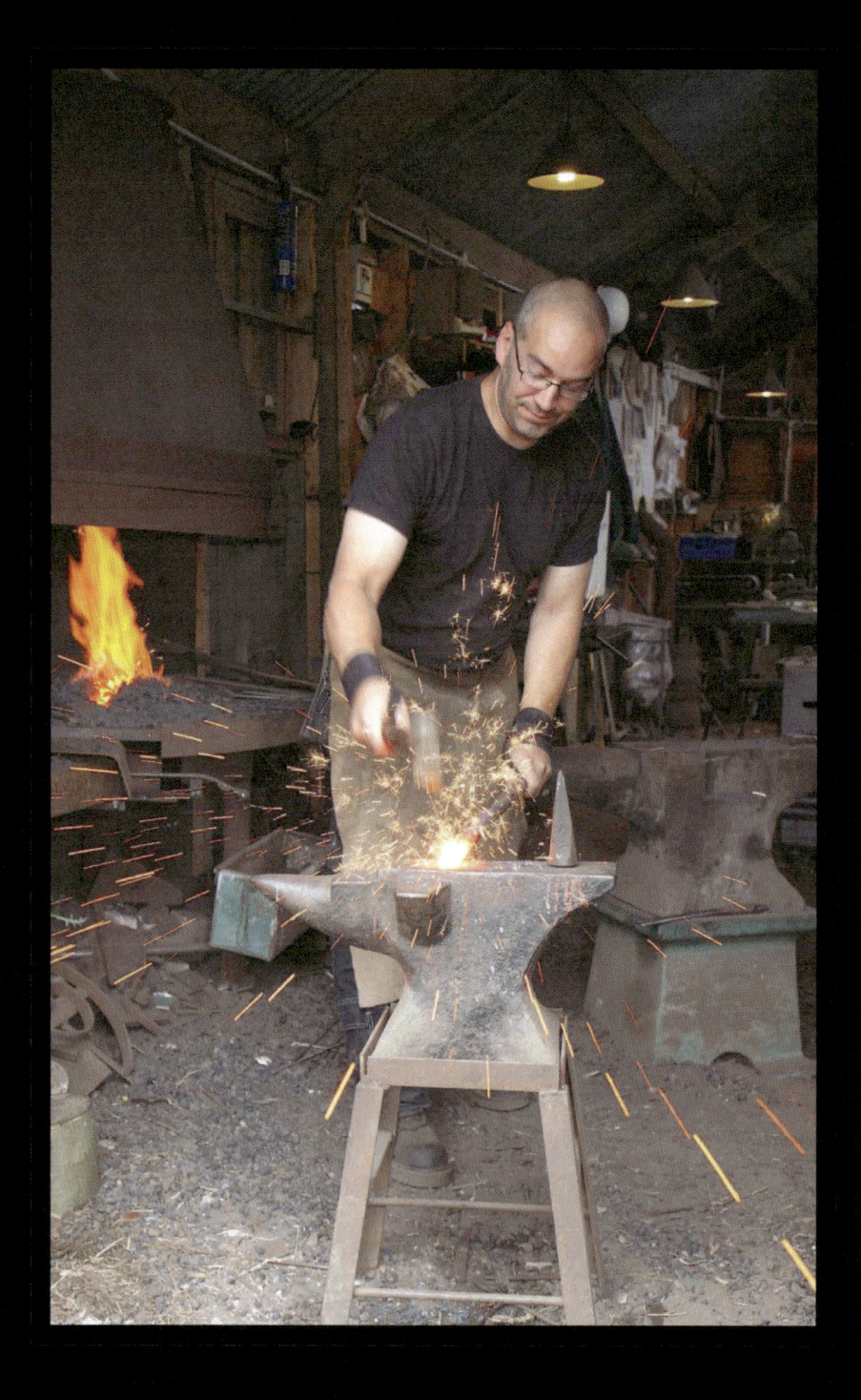

The Feast of Saint Clement

St Clement or 'Old Clem' as he was often referred to was said to have been a medieval saint whose symbol was an anvil and legend has it that he was martyred by being thrown overboard a ship tied to an anchor. The feast goes back hundreds of years and seems to have been popular with dockyard workers who celebrated with explosions of gunpowder on the anvil and lavish feasts for blacksmith and apprentice alike. This tradition seemed consigned to history but has made a comeback in a few locations around the UK.

Left: Illustration by Mike Kelly

Blacksmith Dave Turner, organiser of last year's feast explained to me that the occasion was not so much about honouring a saint: "As a group, Smiths or glass workers or doctors need these shared events and rituals to cement their sameness and togetherness. We work on our own and it can get lonely and induce insularity. Getting together for this shared feast is important to bind us and let us know we are not on our own. We can have a moan, share the hardships and most importantly share information and help."

In the process of writing this article, I was encouraged to find this growing unity and interest in the art on both sides of the Atlantic, but my curiosity grew as to the fate of Giles, the blacksmith whose workshop gave me inspiration to set up my own. Having lost touch when he moved from Sussex, I tracked him down through the magic of social media. I was delighted to find that he was still smithing, still producing artistic and traditional work and working with other like-minded blacksmiths. Where? Santa Fe, New Mexico!

Right: Photo by Andy Meany

Above: Tom Zimmer - An ecological farmer and blacksmith living and working in Alaska with his family.

"As a family farm (Calypso Farm and Ecology Center) we produce vegetables for our community and provide educational programs to help connect folks to their food sources and to learn homesteading skills. Farming encompasses many skills and I was first introduced to blacksmithing when a local farrier and metalworker offered to make us a farm entrance sign and gates. It did not take long for me to see the many utilitarian aspects of blacksmithing. The ability to fix tools was great but the ability to modify/alter tools to your needs was truly eye opening. I am fascinated by it as it allows me to create a tool but it requires me to loosen up and add form to that function.

Blacksmithing has much history and myth about it and people are drawn to the anvil. You can approach it from the science of metallurgy, through art and functionality all the way to the finesse of hammer control. Recently I had the great fortune to go to Maine and attend two wonderful classes at the New England School of Metal Work (NESM). I was interested in learning more about tool making, delving into the world of tool steels. During the first class (Tool making for the Blacksmith) we made hammers, chisels, punches, tongs, scribes and learned how to heat treat. I was very happy with my tools, they were not elegant like the teachers creations but I will improve on this with time. They were however very functional and I used the hammer to forge all of the tools in the second class (Tools of the Trade —Timber Framing tools; axes, draw knives, dividers, mortising chisels and log dogs).

Blacksmithing was historically an apprenticed trade and I feel lucky to be gathering experience and knowledge from the many gifted metal workers out there. I have met blacksmiths from all over, male and female, old and young and they have always been so gracious to open up their smithies to show me skills. So here is yet another wonderful attribute of the trade, building community and sharing traditions."   Tom.

The Forge at Mark Cross in Sussex was comprised of a series of snaking wooden sheds, dimly lit and with an earth floor. Giles Blakeley, himself a Master Blacksmith, trained apprentices and took on full time and part time workers like myself. The work comprised of restoration work including old railings, gates, lighting and other architectural metalwork, but also the design and fabrication of new pieces.

Giles since moved to Winchester and eventually to Hawaii and then Santa Fe, New Mexico where he still works in metal and has also become a master carpenter. (www.gilesironworks.com)

Above: Giles Blakeley at Mark Cross Forge - Photo by Tom Acciarini

A Study Visit To Gränsfors Bruk Axe Factory, Bergsjö, Sweden

In 2008 I travelled to Sweden to take a short course in tool and axe making at the world renowned Gränfors Bruk factory where high quality hand made tools have been produced since 1902. I spent a week forging laminated blades using centuries old techniques and making the tools necessary to finally make a carpenters axe. The axe has a blade made from a piece of hard tool steel, fire-welded into the body, making it a tough and sharp axe which can also be used as an accurate carving tool, much as Viking boat makers would have.

Top right, the workshop complete with an array of templates and tools for axe making.
Top left, 5th generation master blacksmith Lars Enander using the power hammer.
Middle left, Master Lars
Middle right, The 60 year old power hammer, still in daily use.
Bottom right, Me with newly forged axe, complete with laminated blade
Bottom left, Master smith Lenhart Petterson forging axe heads on a power hammer dating from the 1920s.

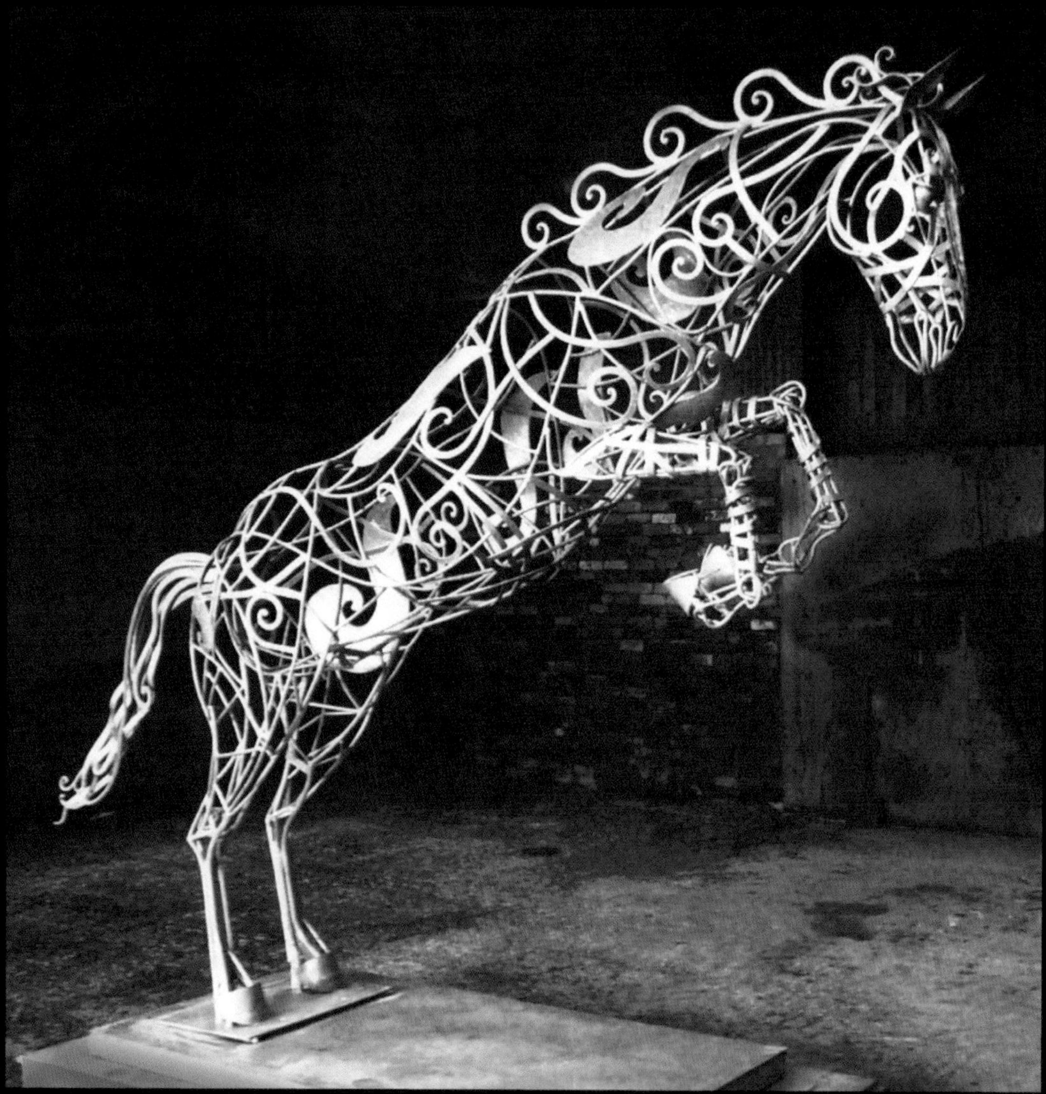

Figurative Sculpture

As a student of psychology in London in the early 1990s, I was lucky enough to spend part of my course on an exchange program in Italy where (as I had done back in the UK) I took far more interest in artistic endeavours than the subject I had chosen to study. This brought me into contact with members of the Mutoid Waste company, a rag-bag assembly of like-minded castaways from society who staged epic public performances and parades in London, Italy and Berlin, building incredible machines from scrap metal, giant sculptures from old cars and trucks, and even artwork out of old Russian Mig fighter jets. As a youth seeing this other world, I was transfixed and as an artist I was in love with the idea of shaping junk into things of beauty. On my return to London I began making much more modest pieces of sculpture using anything I could find, eventually receiving commissions from people who saw my work. Needing more space, I asked a local steel fabricator if I could rent a corner of his workshop and eventually ended up working for him for 3 years, learning to weld and shape steel and other metals and making sculpture as a sideline.

Something about the transformative magic of making art out of pieces of metal led me down the route of figurative sculpture. While I can admire some abstract work as well as accepting that it is much more in vogue, it's something I've never been able to or wanted to do. Neither do I seek to copy nature, making models of things I see. Perhaps my grounding in making art from recycled parts enabled me to see new and strange forms emerge from the material, but they would always be recognisable even if somehow distorted or different.

Some forms seem to appeal more than others. Due to the nature of the material I use and the methods I employ, many of my larger pieces are a kind of framework mesh, lacking the overt solidity of bronze or stone and this can give an ethereal quality and a lightness that is at odds with the size of a piece. I have always been fascinated by the workings of artworks, from the rough sketches of great masters to the armatures or support structures made for the creation of sculptures and in some way, in my own work, I like the workings to be seen.

Opposite: Leaping Horse Sculpture 2013

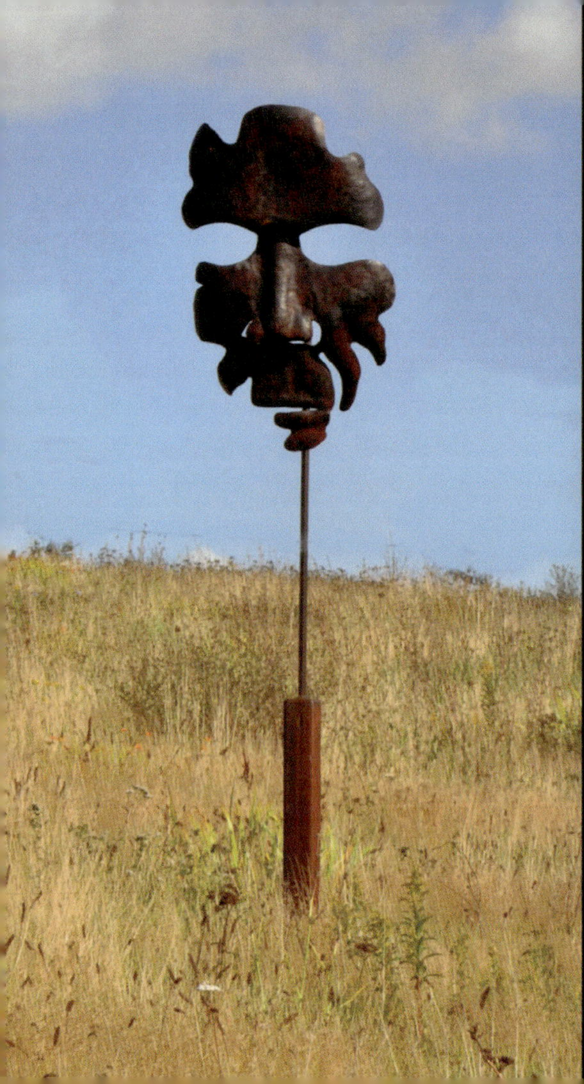

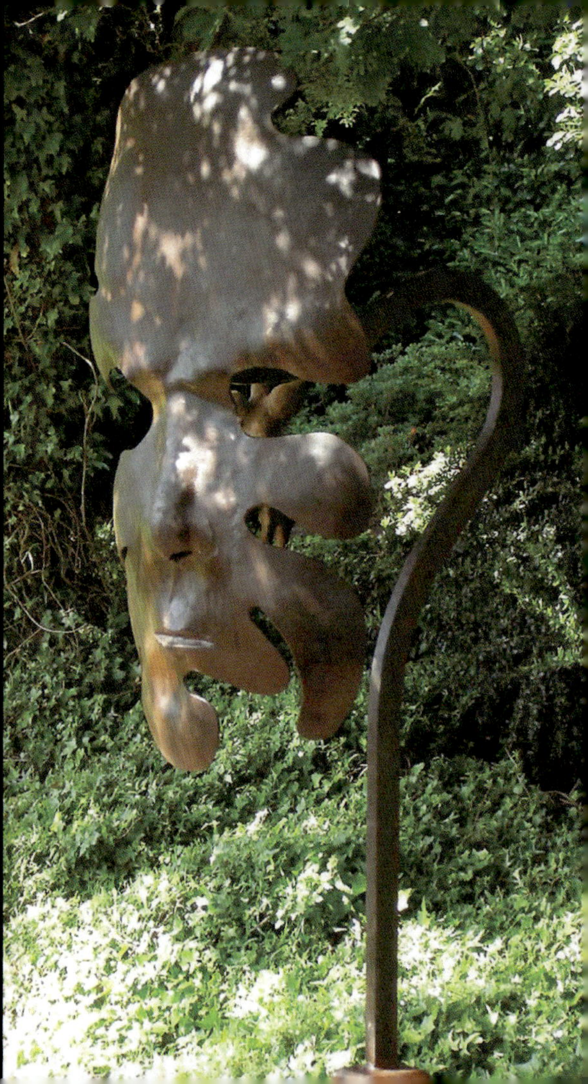

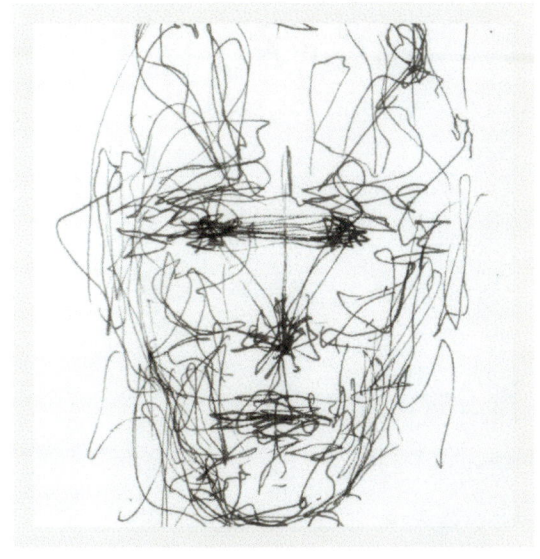

I have often explored the features of the face generally rather than in the form of portraiture.

Opposite Left: Liquid I 2011, oxidised steel.

Opposite Right: Liquid II 2012, oxidised steel.

Top Left: Small Gargoyle 1998 recycled steel pieces.

Top Right: Drawing of a face 1997, lines imagined in wirework.

Left: Sketch 2010, oxidised and forged steel.

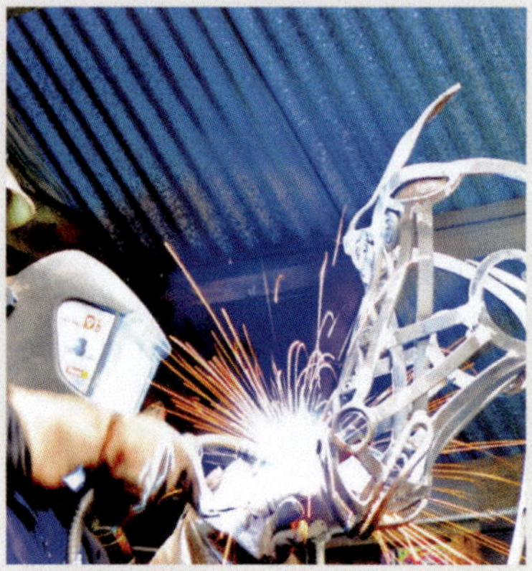

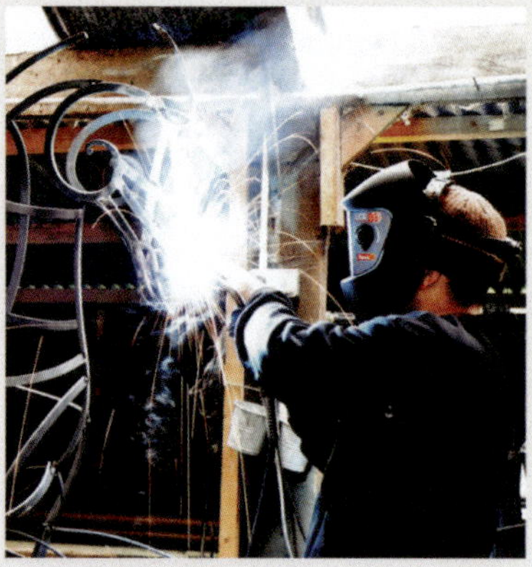

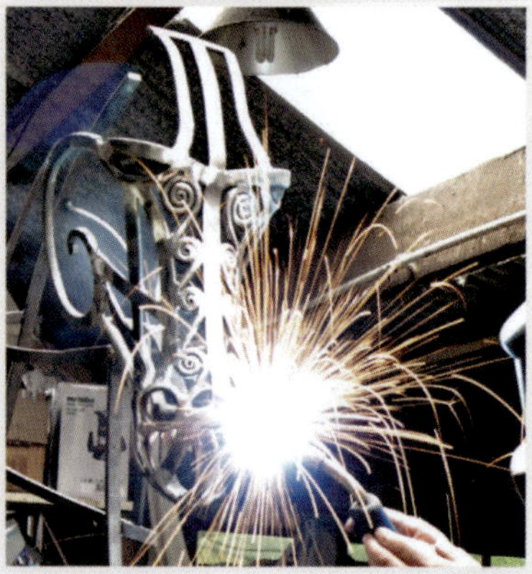

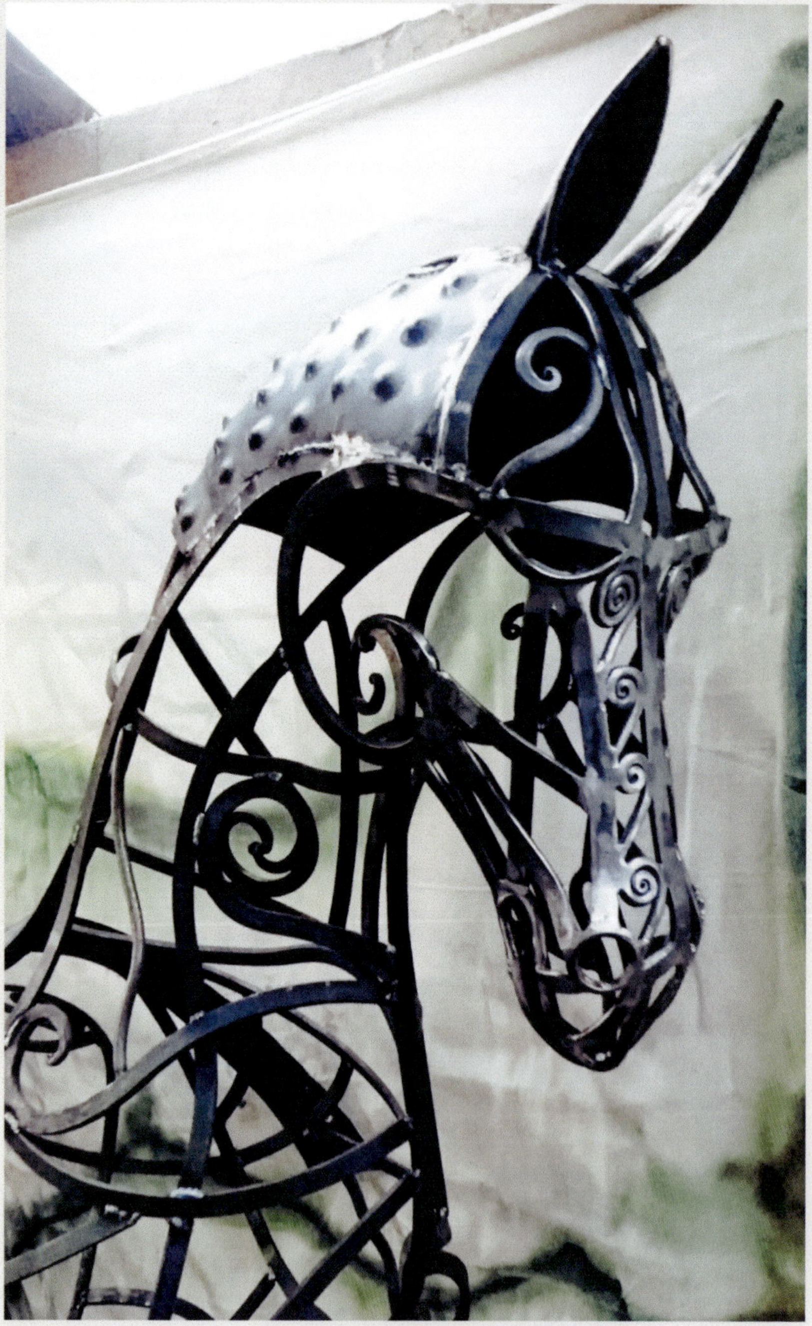

Opposite and above: A work in progress. Ancient Phoenician Chariot with 2 horses 2016
Commissioned by the Oriental Museum in Durham to coincide with the opening of an exhibition on ancient Lebanon.

The sculpture is based on a mixture of sources, from hieroglyphs to ancient scrolls as well as surviving Egyptian artefacts. The finished piece, however will also have considerable artistic licence. The whole sculpture will sit outside the museum and will be life sized.

The chariot will be open so that viewers can interact with it and stand on the back in charioteer poses! It is hoped that the chariot will also be wheelchair accessible.

Usually working in steel, I decided to try the medium of cast bronze and see if I could apply the same lightness. These three pieces are relatively flat, keeping the process simple. I carved a basic facial shape in wood and then cast it in negative in plaster of Paris, which I then layered with heated casting wax. Removing this from the mould I could then further work the wax and repeat the process three times, in each instance treating the wax differently, applying some different textures and details.

I took the waxes to Castle Fine Art Studios in North Wales where I watched them being cast into bronze via the ancient lost wax process. There I learnt techniques of finishing the metal with the use of chemicals and heating, to produce colouration and patina.

I like the permanence of bronze as well as its ability to reproduce the finest detail faithfully. I was amazed to see my own finger prints transferred from the wax into the metal.

Right: Dream I, 2012 Cast Bronze

Opposite: Dream II and Dream III 2012 Patinated Cast Bronze

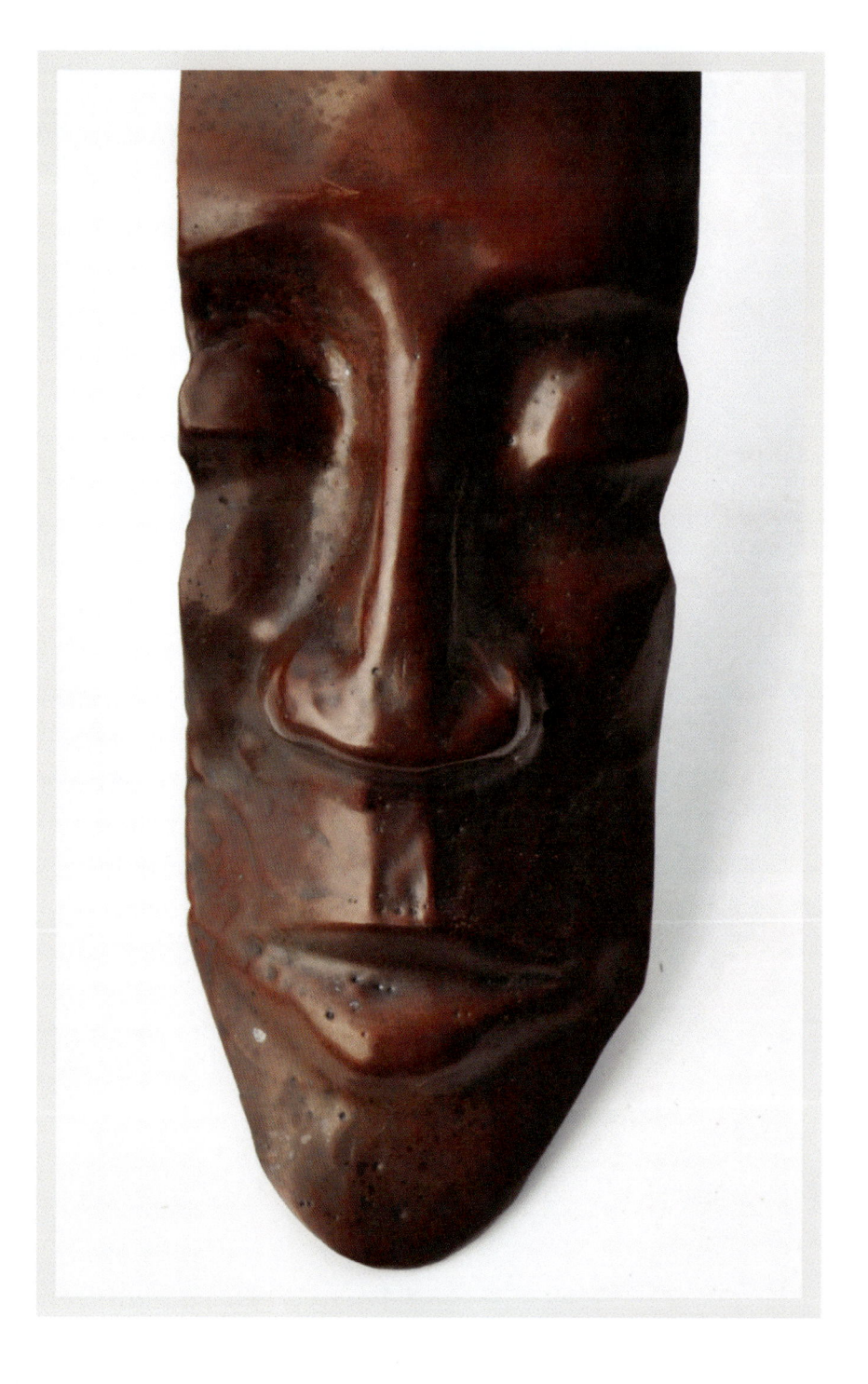

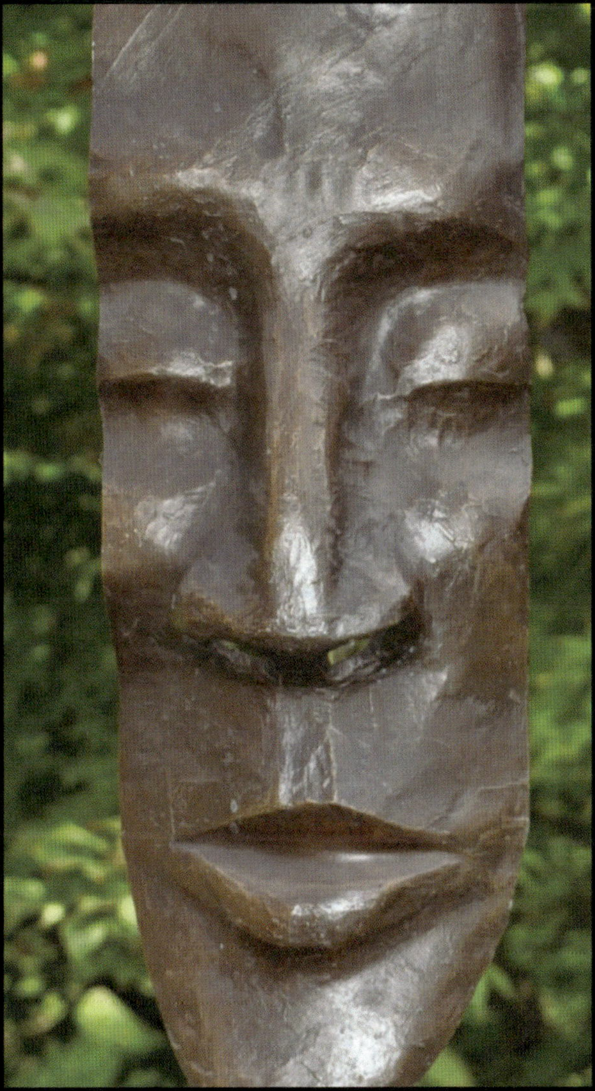
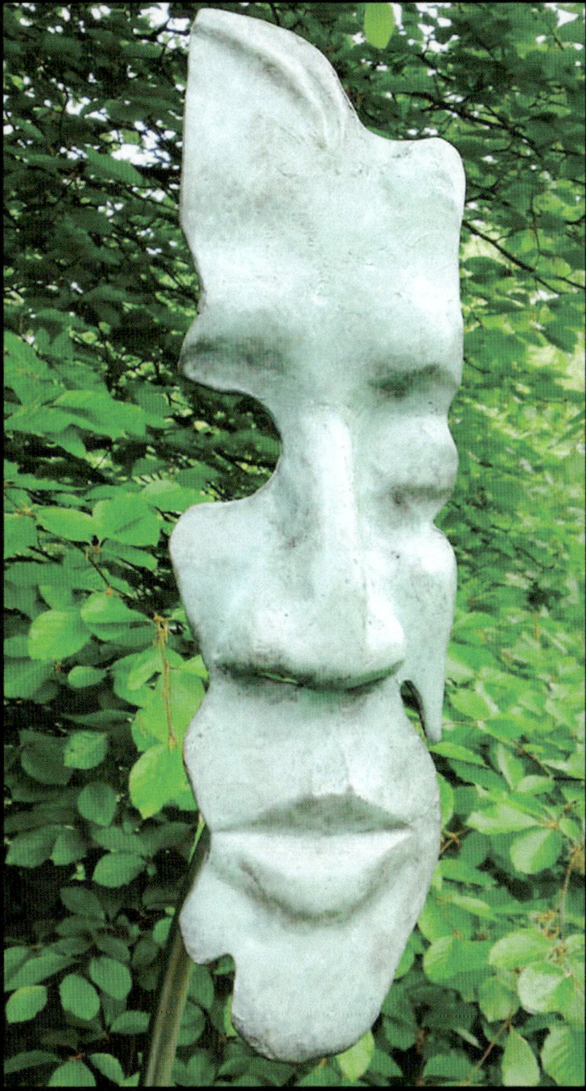

A sense of achievement comes with the creation of any sculpture that has presence. It is something that only really shows itself when the sculpture is positioned in the landscape or setting and is hard to design or plan for. Sometimes a piece instantly has presence and other times a piece has to be worked and reworked until the right feel is achieved. It can also be hard to know when you have got it and occasionally this can take some time. I often need to go away from a piece and come back to see it with fresh eyes.

Right: Prometheus 1998, forged polished and lacquered steel. This is a piece which I worked and reworked over several years until I was happy with the result. As it was not a commission piece, I was able to experiment with techniques, textures and ideas. It sold to a private collector in 2010.

Opposite: Fallow Deer 2013 at a private estate in The Lake District. The surrounding countryside was landscaped in the manor of Capability Brown and deer often come to within a short distance of this sculpture. I was lucky enough to catch this image at dawn with some mist in the valley.

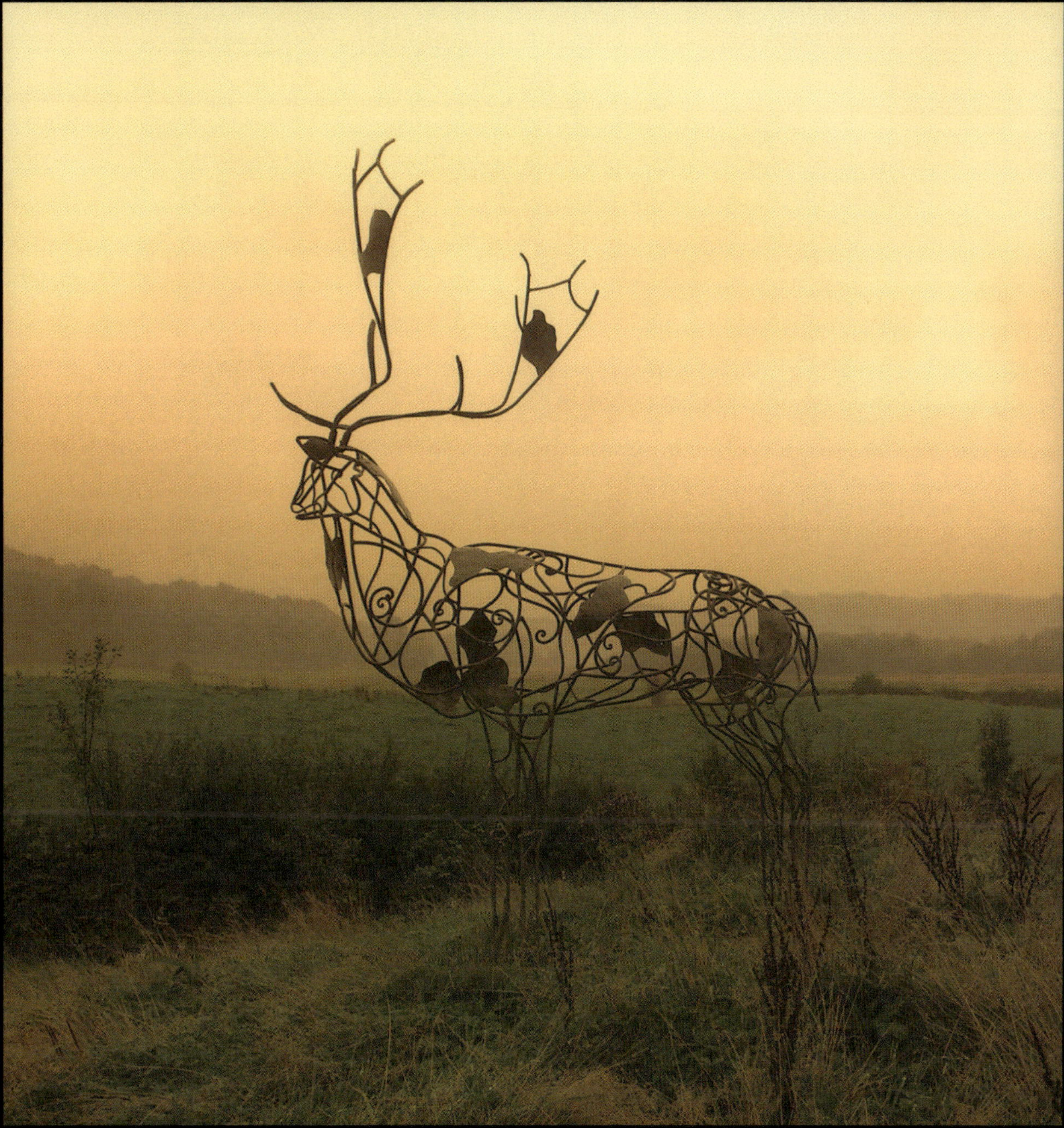

Right: Stag 2013
This is a slightly different version of the deer sculpture, pictured here in my wild garden in Cheshire. Weather changes the appearance and effect of sculpture and this has to be considered when locating a piece which may rarely see sunlight, for example in a dim woodland setting, or may be exposed to bright sunshine. This can influence how I finish a piece and to some extent how it is constructed, often in terms of how dense or light the ironwork is made. This piece is now in a garden in the Cotswolds.

Opposite: Wind Sculpture 2012
Galvanised wrought iron, stainless steel and oxidised wrought iron. Private garden, Nantwich, Cheshire.

As a newcomer to wind sculptures I was keen to achieve something far less geometric and symmetrical than I had seen elsewhere, but this carried the obvious challenge of getting the balance right so that it would move nicely. The sculpture is around 5m high in total and represents a swirl of crows and leaves which gently rotate in a random spiral. Lower down there are leaves which gradually become more bird-like as they go up, becoming 5 crows at the top.

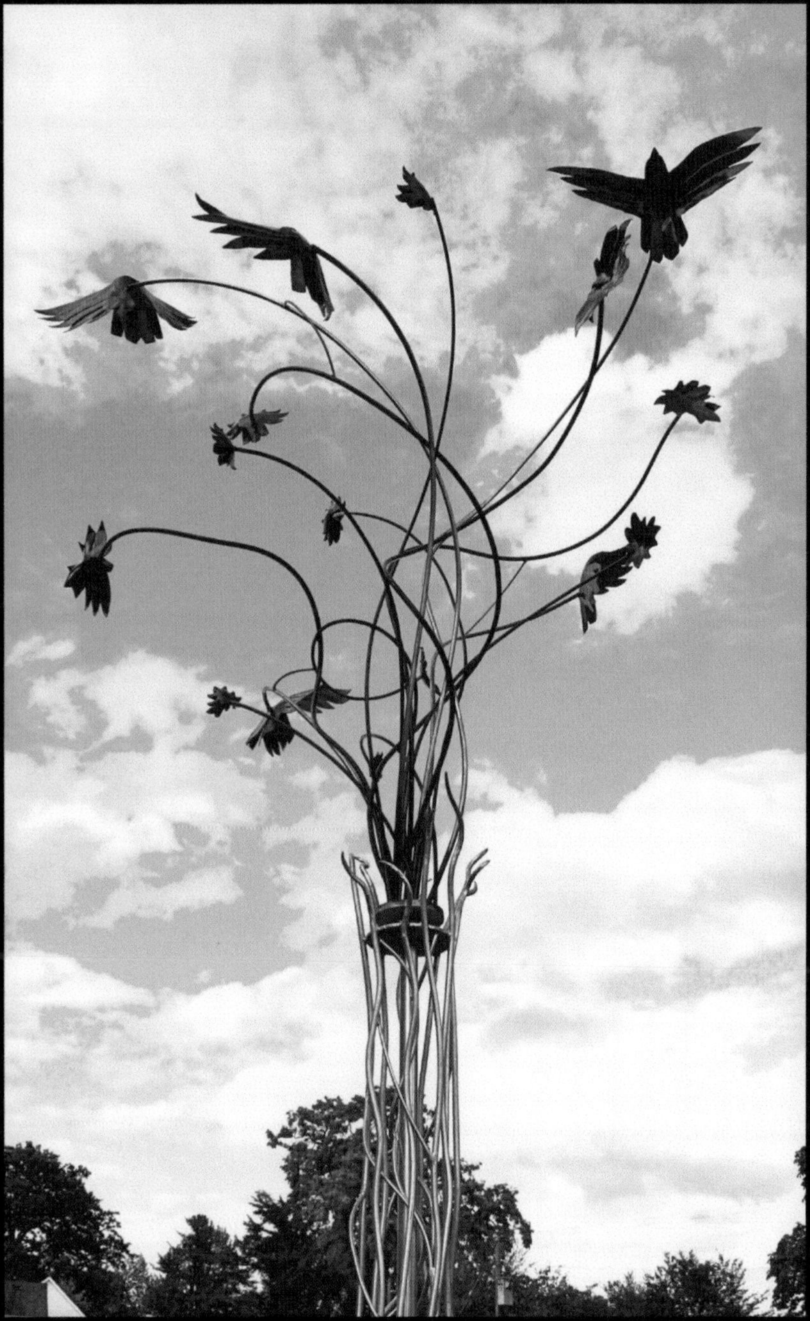

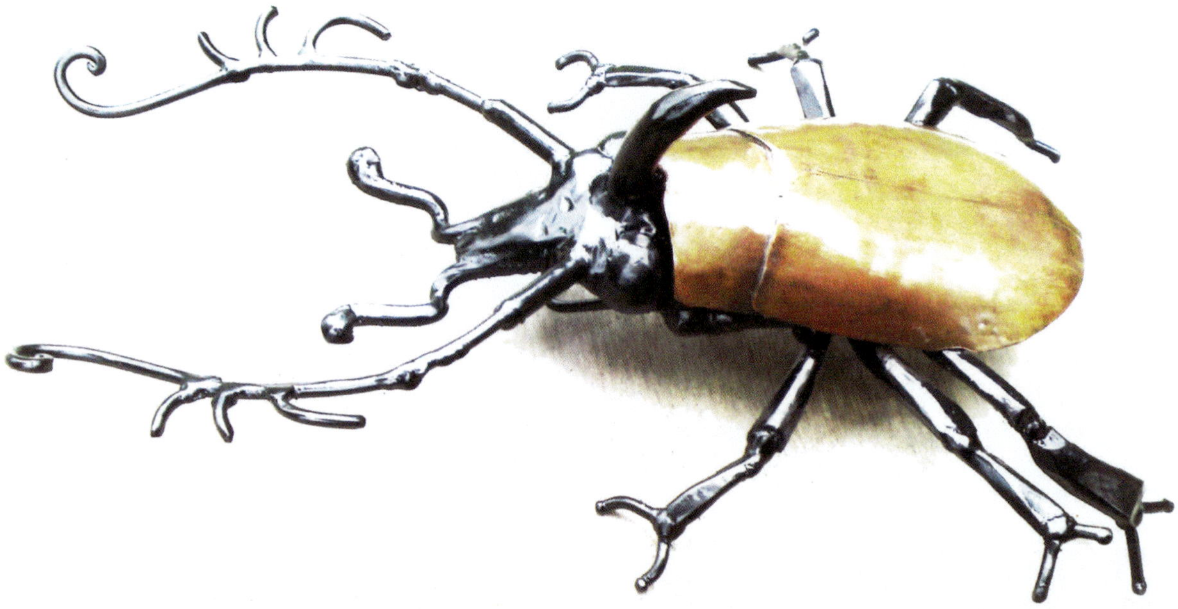

Insect Sculpture

I'm not sure where my preoccupation with the world of invertebrates stems from. All I can be sure of is that it long precedes my interest in sculpture. On discovering at the age of 8 that the British Museum held a treasure trove of spiders that were not on public display, I wrote to them asking if I could get behind the scenes. My mother took me down to London and I got my private viewing of specimens brought back by Darwin and countless other bizarre arachnids. I suppose this could have led me to science, but I was always more interested in the look of them than the technical detail.

Metal seems to suit itself well to making insect sculpture as in many cases these little beasts seem to be armoured and articulated, mirror finished or plated and with appendages more like some form of tooling than something biological. I enjoy working with small details and I usually end up creating my own creatures based on observation rather than trying to copy real insects.

Occasionally though, a particular insect appeals and I can see a way to recreating it in metal, as in the case of the hawthorn shield bug (p.66). When asked to make some insect pieces for the Woodland Trust in Scotland, I was obliged to represent the fauna of the local environment, but this proved to be a great bonus. The Sabre Wasp (p.65) or Ichneumon present in that part of the UK turns out to be more bizarre than anything I could have imagined, with a wood boring drillbit on its abdomen and incredible patterns on its back.

I find that using different metals (and sometimes even wood) can help to capture the variety of textures and colours in the insect world. Stainless steel has the permanence and bright finish that will stand out for years in the outdoors, while copper will gradually change and evolve, eventually turning greeny blue. Mild steel can be galvanised for a shiny finish which can also be dulled with acid to grey. Sometimes paints can add accents or enhance small areas of a piece.

Opposite: Beetle 2007 - Legs and body in mild steel with black gloss paint finish, carapace in copper.

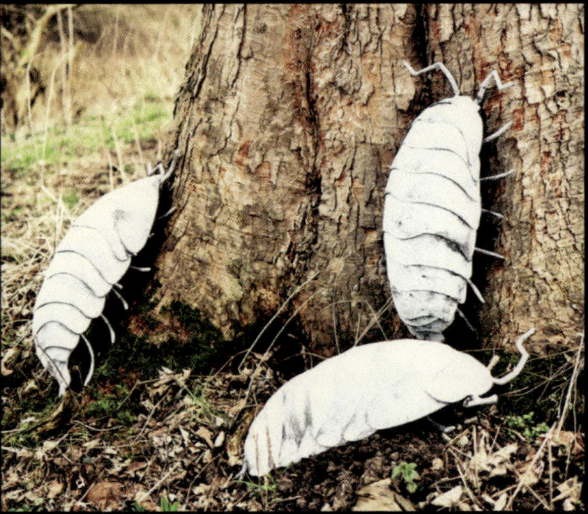

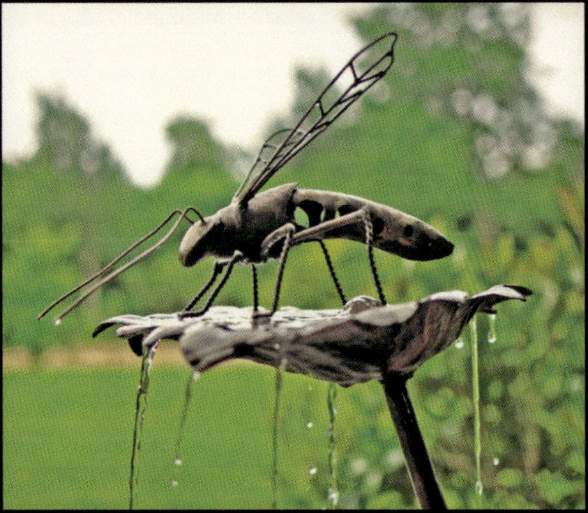

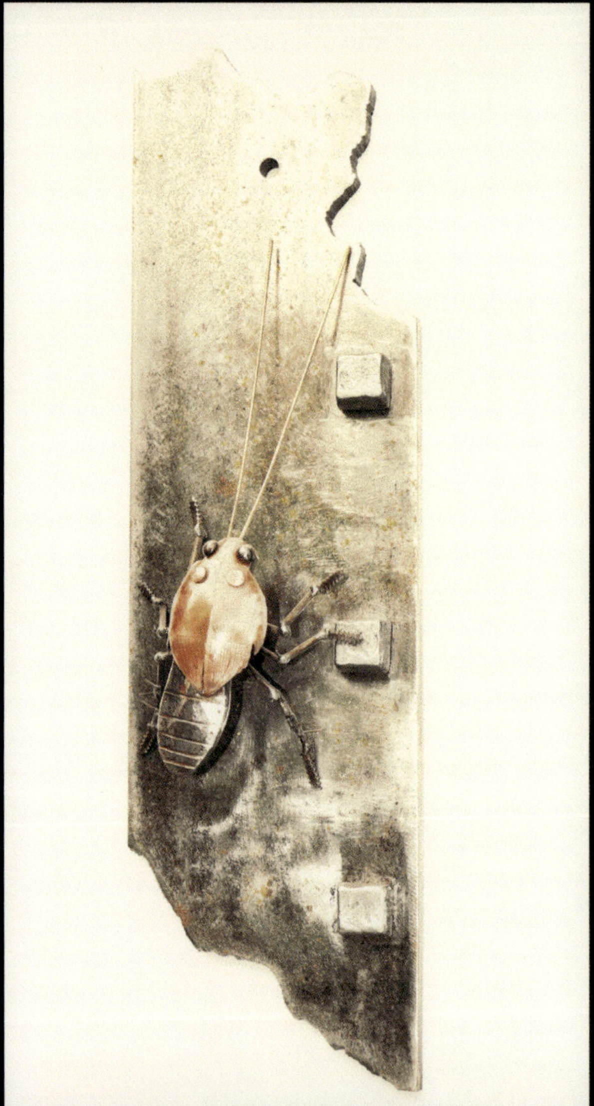

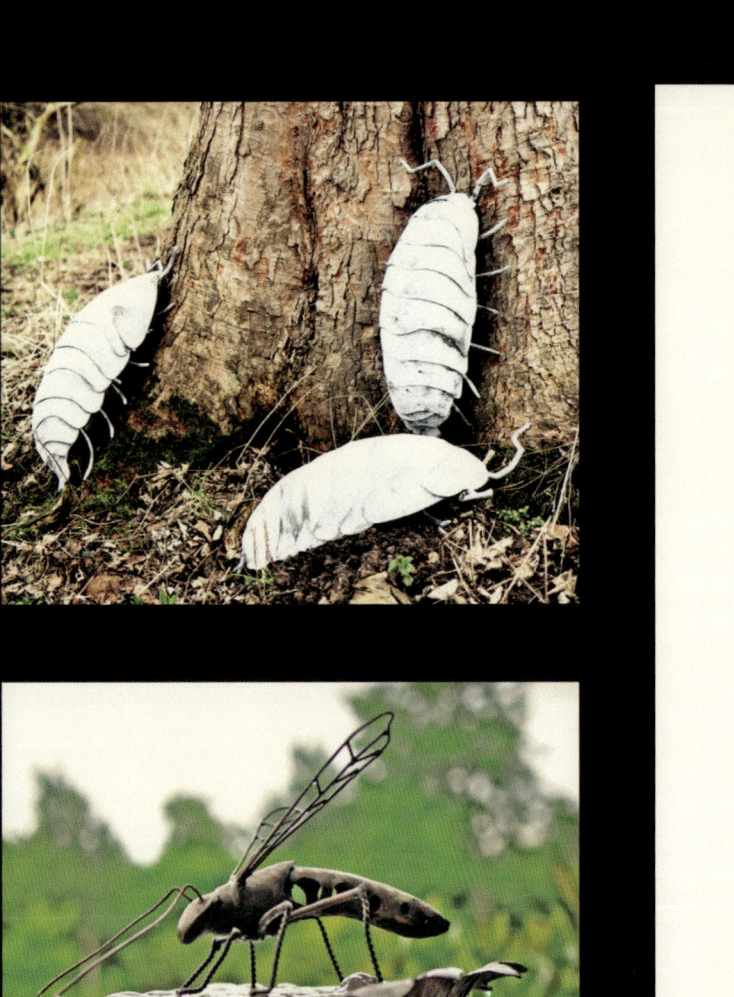

Opposite Top Left: Woodlice 2014
These large steel and galvanised woodlice were made for the Woodland Trust site at Butterbean Wood in East Lothian, Scotland, and were eventually positioned climbing round a tree trunk. Here pictured near my workshop.

Opposite Bottom Left: Water Feature detail 2015
This copper water feature was accented by an insect detail. The creature is of my own invention.

Opposite Right: Long Beetle 2005
Some finishes are not designed for the outdoors and this beetle uses natural steel, with only a light wax so is for indoor display. The carapace is copper.

Left: Sabre Wasp 2014
The ichneumon wasp looks more like something from a tropical climate, but lives in the UK, Scotland included, and bores into wood to lay eggs in the grubs of other insects! This was positioned high up a pine tree in Butterbean Wood, Scotland. The legs are in copper and the body is in gloss panted steel. The wings and antennae are in stainless steel. Pictured here at my workshop before the trip north.

Right: Hawthorn Shield bug 2015
The hawthorn leaf and blossom detail was made in forged mild steel, the blossom with a touch of white paint. The bug was made in copper with verdigris details. The patina on the bug will change gradually over time. Private garden, Cheshire UK.

Opposite Top Left: Dragonfly 2013
Stainless steel. Pictured at Arley Hall in Cheshire. This piece is designed to go either on land or can be placed in a pond with the rock plinth submerged.

Opposite Top Right: Insect landing on a flower 2012
Pictured at Hidcote Manor Garden. Galvanised steel and paint detail. I have made many similar pieces, designed to fit into decorative floral borders.

Opposite Bottom Left: Fly 2012
Stainless steel. Made partly from recycled items including several spoons and two small milk jugs and some stainless steel bolts.

Opposite Bottom Right: Insect on cow parsley 2010
A small and delicate piece which sways in the wind. Galvanised steel with paint details.

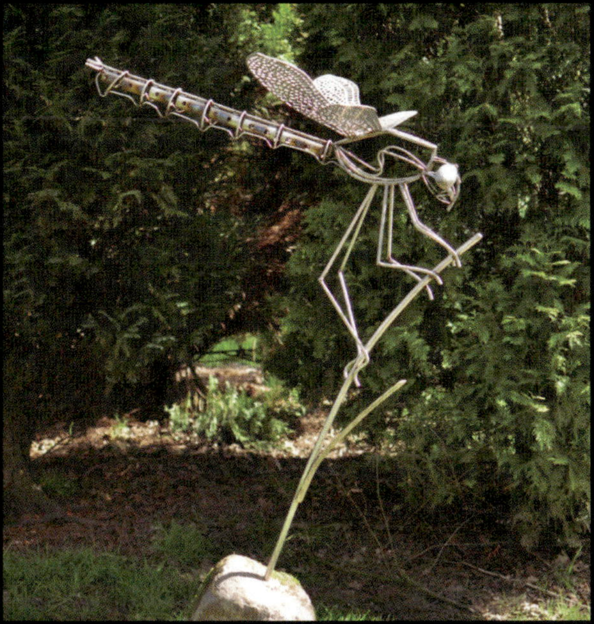
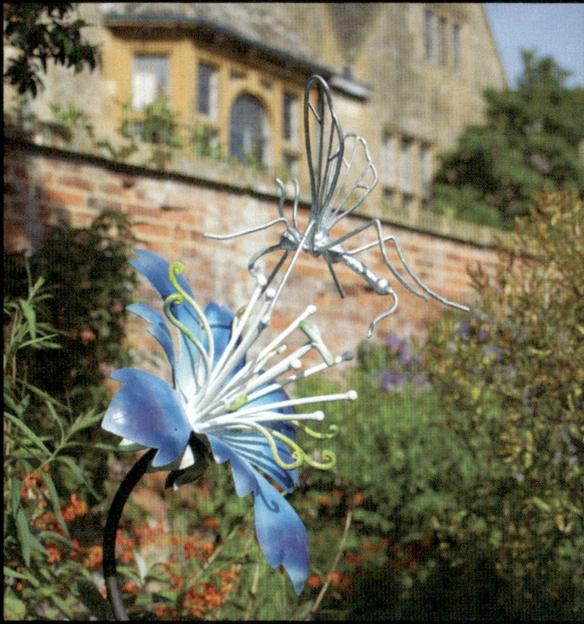
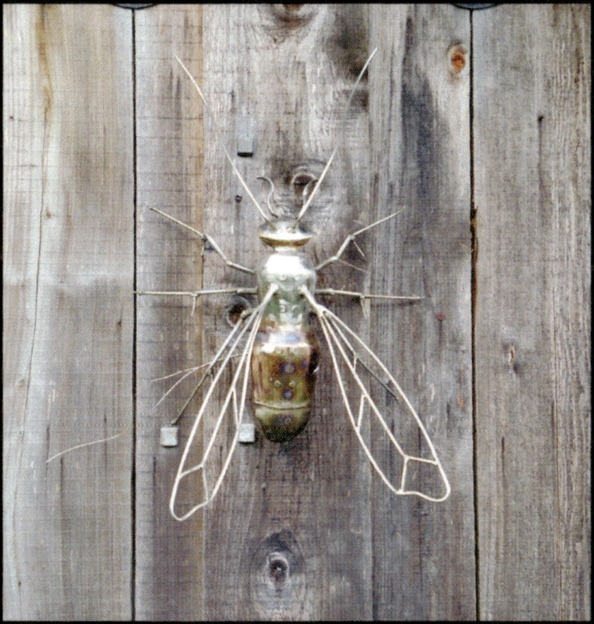
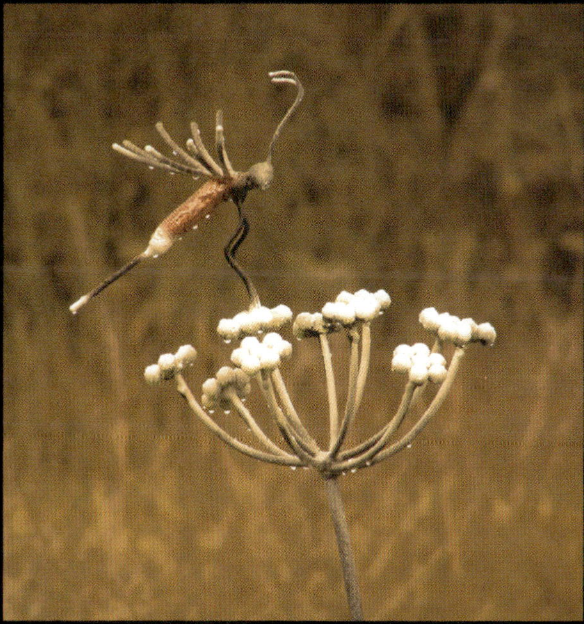

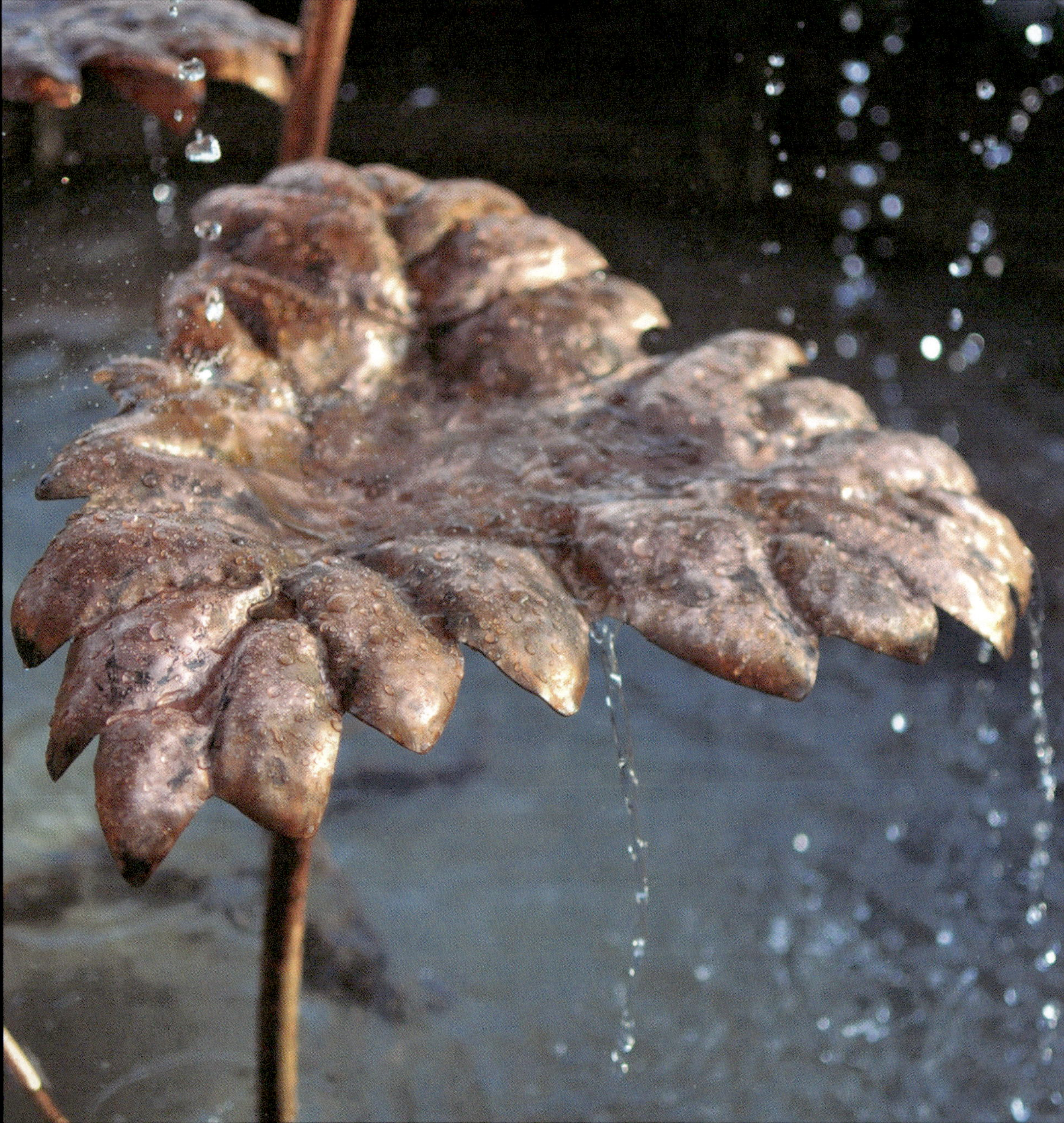

Copper and Water

After decades of working with wrought iron, banging and bashing, bending and shaping, to discover copper work was a delight. It is soft and supple, delicate and forgiving, light and strong. A whole realm of possibilities was opened up to me for sculpture, but also for the creation of sculptural water features giving a whole new dynamic to a piece.

Copper lends itself to sculpture as good detail can be produced by many techniques. It can be punched, drilled, bent, engraved and stretched. It can be worked hard which gives a 'beaten' look or it can be annealed or softened using heat, and it can then be shaped very easily. It is also relatively easy to solder and braise copper without the joints being ugly or too visible.

Apart from making things in copper, I enjoy creating the tools for the job, which are often very simple formers, some in steel and some in wood. I have made doming blocks of various sizes as well as many punches and chisels, all to achieve particular shapes and patterns. Traditional reppousé work can also involve the use of a leather bag filled with beads, against which the copper can be hammered out.

Copper is a great material for water features and fountains, evolving over time into a stunning verdigris patina. Its common use in plumbing also enables it to be piped easily and it holds pressure well for pumping and for reservoirs.

It is easy to overlook copper as a medium for sculpture, with bronze seen as its superior cousin, but it has unique qualities and its own methods and techniques of working that make it appealing. There is also a wealth of scrap copper items out there to be re-used, from plumbing pipes, hot water tanks, to electrical wire, it can nearly always be re-worked into something new.

Opposite: Detail from a fountain 2013. The leaves were based on giant gunnera, and the water had to be carefully directed to flow evenly from the leaves.

Top Right: Gunnera Fountain 2013
Georgian Manor House, Cumbria. This fountain was designed so that the water pumped up through the central stem would trickle down to each of the four lower leaves and then down into the water.

The larger leaves were challenging to form due to their size. I had to heat and cool sections at a time to work on them, and the only former large enough to beat them on was a huge oak stump outside my workshop.

Bottom Right: Sunflower with bug 2015.
This was made from the base of an old hot water cylinder which after decades of use in a house, was still perfectly good raw material to use for sculpture. This was a small piece to hang on a garden wall.

Opposite: Gunnera Fountain 2013
View showing the rolling landscape designed in the manner of Capability Brown. The stonework of the fountain is a Victorian addition.

Part of the art of water features is the sound. It is important that it be a constant soothing trickle like that of a stream, rather than a tapping sound like rain on a tin roof.

Right: Small garden water feature 2015, Copper.
This feature was placed above a reservoir tank that I submerged to ground level. A grid was made for the top which was then covered in stones so that the water could trickle through to be pumped back up through the central stem. This was commissioned for a private garden in Nantwich, Cheshire.

Opposite Left: Copper light fittings 2014.
Commissioned for a Manor House in Cumbria. The owner wanted a slightly Deco style but that would also be sympathetic to the period of the property. Here they are seen shiny and new, but they will age darker and eventually will go verdigris.

Opposite Right: Damselfly pond sculpture 2015
The damselfly is made entirely from copper, with a small amount of paint detail to the wings. I had to reinforce the 'grass' stem with a bar of stainless steel as copper might not be strong enough to withstand the weather. The stem gives a light springiness which allows a little movement. Private garden pond in Nantwich, Cheshire. Insect size is about 1m in length.

73

Over the years I have spent producing artistic metalwork, the books that have always caught my eye have been collections of other people's work. Though I started with a stack of how-to manuals, I always found that there was no substitute for messing about at the forge, or watching an expert.

I chose not to attempt to produce yet another manual here. I think there may be enough out there already, and I hope like me, that you would prefer to stroll through a gallery of work, learning a little about my inspirations and methods and the path I have taken.

Thanks for reading. If you enjoyed this book, please consider leaving a review on Amazon.
www.stuntcrow.com | www.davidfreedmansculpture.com